The School of Self-Knowledge

THE COLUMBA SERIES

1. ON CONTEMPLATING GOD. William of St. Thierry
2. ON JESUS AT TWELVE YEARS OLD. St. Aelred of Rievaulx
3. THE SCHOOL OF SELF-KNOWLEDGE.
4. ON THE NATURE AND DIGNITY OF LOVE. William of St. Thierry
5. LETTER TO MY SISTER. Saint Aelred of Rievaulx.
6. THE STEPS OF HUMILTY. St. Bernard.
7. LETTERS OF SPIRITUAL DIRECTION. Bossuet.

A Symposium from Mediaeval Sources

The School of Self-Knowledge

Translated from the Latin by
GEOFFREY WEBB AND ADRIAN WALKER

London
The Saint Austin Press
MMI

Nihil Obstat: JOHANNES M. T. BARTON, S.T.D., L.S.S.
Imprimatur: E. MORROGH BERNARD, *Vic. Gen.*
Westmonasterii, die 26a Mai, 1955

The Saint Austin Press
296 Brockley Road
London
SE4 2RA
Tel +44 (0)20 8692 6009
Fax +44 (0)20 8469 3609
Email: books@saintaustin.org
Website: www.saintaustin.org

ISBN 1901157 57 1

First published by Mowbrays in 1956

Design and typography of this edition © The Saint Austin Press, 2001.

All rights reserved.
A CIP record of this book is available.

"The publishers have made considerable efforts to trace the current copyright holders of this work, first published nearly 50 years ago, but have been unable to do so. If they have unwittingly infringed copyright, they will be happy to honour any reasonable claims from copyright holders who contact them in writing at the above address."

Printed by Newton Design & Print Ltd, London, UK.   www.newtondp.co.uk

INTRODUCTION

THE extent of Saint Bernard's influence on the spiritual authors of the twelfth and thirteenth centuries is something which strikes everyone who reads through the various volumes of works attributed to him by later generations. Over and above his own considerable output, no less than 120 prose compositions and more than fifty poems have been ascribed to him since his death in 1153, and the work of tracing the *de facto* authors of these works still goes on. Since Saint Bernard's disciples were faithful exponents of his doctrine, their writings may be placed without any doubt in the Cistercian school. But it is often difficult to see how the Middle Ages could attribute these works to the master. Although substantially Bernardine in content, their mode of expression has begun to change even before the end of the twelfth century.

This change can be traced to two main causes. Firstly, the spiritual direction of layfolk becomes more widespread in the Cistercian order at this time, and would seem naturally to demand short, condensed meditations for the use of people in the world. These begin to replace the longer treatises and commentaries of earlier monastic authors, not only outside but also within the monasteries. Secondly, and quite certainly due to influences from the Netherlands and the Rhineland, the style of spiritual teaching becomes more and more decorated with remarkable anecdotes, pious lives, miracles, and private revelations. Thus we find that the '*Exordium Parvum*,' a brief, factual history of the origins of the Cistercian order, is expanded by Conrad of Eberbach into an '*Exordium Magnum*,' containing many an edifying (and later) tradition about the lives of those early monks.

It already foreshadows, in fact, the enormously popular 'Dialogue on Miracles' of the Cistercian Caesar of Heisterbach, and shows how the order, with its great abbey of Villers in Brabant, participated in the current which led to the mysticism of Eckhardt and his Flemish school.

The three authors represented in this little book are all Cistercians of the late twelfth and early thirteenth centuries. As one would expect in such *ex professo* treatments of the subject of self-knowledge, they keep to the traditional doctrine as laid down by Saint Benedict and developed by Saint Bernard. The seventh chapter of the Rule, entitled 'On the steps of humility,' urges the monk to aim at achieving the knowledge which makes him esteem himself for what he is. Not only must a monk be able to accept the truth about himself from the lips of others, but he must realize and acknowledge that what they say is true. The Rule never envisages an introspective analysis of self, but insists rather on self-knowledge as the indispensable basis of the spiritual life. It is Saint Augustine's prayer, '*Noverim me, noverim te*' developed through centuries of monastic lives, but eminently valid for the layman too.

But although their teaching is traditional, our three authors are not without their share of later influences. One notices a debt, not only to the Cistercian fathers, but to the school of Saint Victor which tended to be more speculative, and to give less emphasis to the rôle of Christ in the soul's journey to God. More secular culture is apparent, and quotations from classical Latin authors become more varied and numerous. This is particularly and understandably the case with Hélinand of Froidmont (1127–1212), for in his long life he had been a scholar and a troubadour, delighting the ear of Philippe Auguste of France with his songs. As a monk he continued to write, both in Latin and French, and his celebrated verses on death provide a key to an interesting aspect of the current development of spirituality. When he requests that Death should pay a visit to his friends 'it is not because I love them less, but because the fear of death is a refining fear.' Death is to remind the bishop of Beauvais that a man's last hour plays hide and seek with him. . . .

It is a later development to throw into relief the joys of heaven by considering the pains of hell. It is something we find in Saint Aelred, writing in 1160, whereas it is absent from Bernard and William of Saint-Thierry who wrote in the first half of the century. We find a similar approach to Hélinand's in the *Meditatio Piissima*, which belongs to the beginning of the thirteenth century. This is the most popular of all the works which the Middle Ages attributed to Saint Bernard, being more widely circulated than any of the works for which the saint was personally responsible. One finds it as late as 1663 in the Meditation Manual of the English College at Lisbon. Nothing is known about the author, whose anonymity may well be due to the fact that he does not propose to offer original doctrine. The meditation is a florilegium, in which the reader familiar with the period will recognize many familiar themes. None the less, the author has some beautiful thoughts to offer, and his prayer to the brother priest recalls Walafrid Strabo's lines 'to a friend in absence.'

The *Domus Interior* belongs to the same period as the *Meditatio Piissima*, and the author's anonymity is again probably attributable to the same cause. In this work, however, one finds the doctrine of self-knowledge schematized into a method of prayer. Such a formulation is not common among the earlier Cistercians, but the prayer as such is a favourite one with them all. Saint Aelred, for instance, calls it 'the prayer of the memory of Christ's benefits,' the Cistercian '*memoria*' referring not so much to things past as to things which are eternally present with God. The memory of Christ's benefits, such as one finds it set forth here, and in the lovely sequence '*Jesu dulcis memoria*,' so long attributed to Saint Bernard, is designed to bring the soul into a present communion with God by means of gratitude and love.

The Latin texts from which these translations have been selected are to be found in the *Migne Patrology* under the following references:

Hélinand de Froidmont, 'Liber de Cognitione Sui,'
P.L. 212, col. 723.
'Meditatio Piissima de cognitione humanae conditionis,'
P.L. 184, col. 485.
'De Conscientia Aedificanda, seu de Interiori Domo,'
P.L. 184, col. 511.

ADRIAN WALKER
GEOFFREY WEBB

Easter 1955

CONTENTS

INTRODUCTION 5

From the *Liber de Cognitione Sui* of Hélinand of Froidmont

1. KNOW THYSELF 11
2. THE BEAUTY OF THE SOUL . . . 14

From the *Meditatio Piissima*

3. THE IMAGE OF GOD 17
4. THE PROMISE OF ETERNAL LIFE . . 21
5. THE PERFECT CHRISTIAN . . . 23
6. ON PRAYER 26
7. THE INCONSTANCY OF THE HUMAN HEART . 30
8. AN EXAMINATION OF CONSCIENCE . . 34
9. THE OLD MAN AND THE NEW . . 38

From the *Domus Interior*

10. THE INNER HOUSE OF CONSCIENCE . . 41
11. THE SEVEN PILLARS OF WISDOM . . 44

THE SCHOOL OF SELF-KNOWLEDGE

CHAPTER I

KNOW THYSELF

It is said that on the tripod of Apollo's oracle at Delphi were written the words 'Know Thyself.'[1] This was no doubt put there for the benefit of those who came to consult the oracle, since it shows the way in which a man may attain to beatitude. We need not suppose that Apollo himself was the author of the phrase. I suspect rather that he borrowed it from elsewhere. To know oneself is to follow the precept which we find in the book of Job—'Thou shalt know that thy tabernacle is in peace, and visiting thy beauty thou shalt not sin.'[2] And the bride in the Canticle is warned: 'If thou know not thyself, O fairest among women, go forth and follow after the steps of the flocks.'[3]

Considering the great usefulness of the words 'Know Thyself,' Juvenal insisted that they held a divine and heavenly meaning, and must certainly have come down from above.[4] Their meaning for us is that all knowledge is futile and all wisdom savourless, if we remain in ignorance of the one thing necessary. What can it profit a man to measure the whole world, if he is unfamiliar with his own nature? Without this knowledge of himself, nothing is of use to a mortal man, nor can anything lead him to salvation. This is the first thing necessary, as it is the only thing necessary, for it teaches a man to fear God, to beware of sin, to love his neighbour, to desire the things of heaven and to detach himself from the world.

The saying is a heavenly one then, and to be attributed to the prophet rather than the oracle ... 'Visiting thy beauty thou shalt not sin.' Now the beauty of man is twofold, for man himself is twofold, as the apostle testifies when he says, 'though our outer nature is wasting away, our inner nature is being renewed every day.'[5] The outward man is the body and the inward man is the soul. In man's outward beauty there are four things to notice. These are the lowliness of its matter, the dignity of its form, the sufferings to which human life is subject, and the inevitability of its passing away. Of the first we read: 'God formed man of the dust from the ground.'[6] Of the second Ovid wrote:

> Although all else that lives bends downwards, looking earthwards,
> He gave to man a countenance uplifted, bidding him
> Behold the heavens, and direct his upright gaze
> Upon the stars.[7]

Of the third we read in the book of Job that 'man is born to labour.'[8] As to the fourth, we can remember God's words to Adam, 'Dust thou art, and unto dust thou shalt return.'[9]

This consideration brings about a fourfold result. Seeing the lowliness of the material out of which we are made, we see how lowly we are in ourselves. Thinking of the dignity of our soul, or our form, we conceive a desire for the eternal kingdom of heaven. Experiencing the sufferings of life, we become compassionate and charitable to our brethren. Realizing that one day body and soul must part company, we conceive the fear of judgement.

The uplifted countenance of man is so designed in order that we may desire to be truly detached from earthly things, and that we may love God above all else. Plato gave thanks to nature that he was born a man, and this is not surprising, for God in creating us has made us beautiful to behold. And to come nearer to our own days, it is said that one of Bernard's monks, when talking with some friends, happened to remark that he never saw anything which did not in some way edify him. This prompted one of his companions to reply, 'What do you find edifying about a toad?' He answered, 'Many things . . . for instance, I have not merited that God should make me a man rather than a toad. Whenever I see a toad I thank God for His kindness in making me, not hideous to look at, but with the beauty of a human form; a creature of nobility instead of a beast. And again, when I see a toad—ugly as it is, disgusting and venomous—I fear lest I should ever become like a toad in my habits, and delivered to hell by reason of the ugliness of my soul.'

Indeed, the human form alone, to say nothing of our other endowments, is an occasion for thanking God greatly. The sufferings which we must abide, being common to all, are likewise something to thank God for, for they are an occasion for striving after brotherly love. The inevitability of death and the dissolution of the body have their use in reminding us of the last judgement.

CHAPTER 2

THE BEAUTY OF THE SOUL

THE inward beauty of man is twofold. There is a natural beauty common to all, and a particular beauty which is special to each, since it depends on the good will of the individual. Man's natural beauty is in that he is a rational soul, immortal, invisible, and not bound by the ties of place. His rationality guards him from giving himself up to the pleasures of the senses, and his immortality warns him against the folly of avarice. Among all the monsters of the world, there is surely none more monstrous than a human body inhabited by a bestial soul. Aristotle and Sallust are agreed that a man who has given himself up to greed and sensuality cannot be considered as anything more than an animal.

Reason has a threefold office—to distinguish between things which are contrary, to reprobate things which are evil, and to choose those which are good. Devils can discern between good and evil, but they cannot choose anything but evil. Therefore the kind of man who chooses that which is evil, knowing full well that it is evil, is little better than a devil. Nothing is further from reason than that the immortal soul of man should covet what is mortal, for the soul, in a little while, must leave behind it all its treasures and go empty-handed into eternity. Nothing is more repugnant than that the invisible soul, whose deeds are done in secret, should delight in boasting or in being praised. The fact that our soul is invisible should persuade us to perform all our acts in secret as far as we may, so that our Father, Who sees what is hidden, may reward us. It is an abuse which almost verges on the black art, to make a pompous show to human eyes of the invisible gifts of wisdom, holiness, or any virtue that may be in us, with which our creator has endowed us.

When we consider how the soul gives life to the body, being in all its parts without being confined exclusively to any one of them, are we not reminded of Saint Paul's words: 'If one member suffers, all suffer together'?[10] Is not this a wonderful lesson in brotherly love? For the members of a body are kept together by one spirit, and all are equal and are bound by the ties of love. Therefore a man who resents the fact that his neighbour is praised, judging himself to be slighted thereby, should see that his own glory, far from being diminished, is increased. The glory of any one member redounds to the honour of the whole body.

Thus far we have spoken of the beauty which is common to all souls by reason of their natural endowments. Now the particular beauty of each soul depends on the will and consists of two things—in doing those things which God desires for us, and in avoiding the things of which we know beyond doubt that He disapproves. The will of God is the rule and measure by which we must adjust our wills. On this showing, a soul's beauty is its holiness, and this holiness consists in a firm and stable purpose and a constant affection for all that is holy. The holy love of God implies a holy hatred of evil. Evil is the occasion of sin, but goodness for us is God Himself and the imitation of God. Holy love and holy fear are like the two eyes of the dove in the Canticle, for the dove is of all birds the most timorous and the most loving. For us, cleanness of heart comes through embracing goodness and fleeing from evil.

We must add that in order to know our own soul we must first know our soul's exemplar, that is God, in Whose image and likeness our soul is made. This is, after all, in the due order of things. The seal in the ring comes before the seal which it imprints in the wax. The idea comes before the expression in which it is phrased. Therefore to Apollo's dictum 'know thyself,' we would add 'but know God first.'

There are seven ways in which our soul resembles God. First, God is a spirit, and so is our soul. God is immortal and invisible—likewise the soul. God is one in substance and in persons three. Our soul too is a unity, with three powers of reason, memory and will. God is present everywhere, and the soul is present in every part of the body. God is intellectual, and the soul for its part is intelligent.

When the human soul knows that God is a spirit, it can see what sort of spirit it is itself. It can begin to see that there is a life of the spirit distinct from that of the flesh. It begins to realize that, in Saint Paul's words, it must not live according to the flesh but according to the spirit.[11] The soul in its simplicity, which is modelled on the unity of God, must realize that it must shun all the complexity of falsehood, and walk uprightly before God. Immortality teaches the soul to fear, not the sufferings of this life, but of the damned in hell. It teaches detachment from the passing pleasures of the world, and instils the desire for those which are, like the soul itself, for all eternity.

CHAPTER 3

THE IMAGE OF GOD

It is true that many men know many things, yet they remain in ignorance of themselves. They are interested in others, but often to the neglect of their own souls. They seek God in outward things when He is waiting to be found within them.

Since this is so I have decided to leave those things which are without, and go to those within; to leave what is base and go up to that which is higher. In this way I shall find out from whence I came and whither I am going. I shall discover what I am and who made me. From the knowledge of myself I shall go onward to the knowledge of God, and the more I know myself, the more I shall know Him. For within myself I find three things—my memory, my reason, and my will (which is to say my love), and by means of these three I can recall the presence of God, I can look upon Him, and I can desire Him and even embrace Him.

When I remember God, He is there in my memory, within me. There I can love Him and delight in Him. My reason then shows me what God is—what He is in Himself, in His angels and His saints, in men and in all His creatures. In Himself He is beyond my understanding, for not only is He the beginning and end of all things, but He Himself had no beginning, nor will He ever have an end. The saints delight in God, and the angels forever seek to gaze on Him. Thus is God delightful and desirable. But in all His creatures He is worthy of admiration and wonder for in His power He creates all, in His wisdom He governs all, and in His great kindness He dispenses the needs of each one of us. In men He is lovable, for He is the God of men and all men are His people. He dwells in them as in a temple, and He loves them, each and every one. And every man who seeks God's presence within him, in his memory, looks upon Him and loves Him, for He is with him.

We must love God because He first loved us, and because He made us in His image and likeness. This He did to mankind alone, and to none of His other creatures. The fact that we are made in God's image means that we have knowledge of the Son of God, and through this knowledge of the Son we have access to God our Father. The Son of God is God's own image and we are so related to the Son of God that we are in truth made in His image. Not only in His image did God make us, but also in His likeness. This implies that the image was to be no static resemblance, but that man, made in God's image, was meant to resemble Christ, God's image, in every feature. We are meant to be like our Lord in all things, in His pure vision of the truth, in His love of peace and in His love of the love of God. Let us then reverence Him ever present within us. Let us embrace Him in our memory and carry Him about with us in our conscience, for our soul is His image by reason of its capacity for receiving Him as a guest and participating in His presence.

The soul, by reason of its powers of self-reflexion, can know and love itself, but this does not make it the image of God. Rather does it image God by reflecting on God, remembering, knowing and loving its creator. When it reflects God thus, it is truly wise. Nothing bears a greater likeness to the high wisdom of God than the human soul with its trinity of powers—memory, knowledge and will—by which it cleaves to the ineffable Trinity above. It would, indeed, be incapable of clinging to its divine model, were

THE IMAGE OF GOD

it incapable of remembering, knowing and loving. It would likewise be unable to lead a life of eternal happiness. Blessed indeed is the soul in which God makes His dwelling. Blessed is he who can say, as Our Lady could say, 'He that made me rested in my tabernacle.'[12] To such a one the repose of heaven could never be denied.

Why is it, then, that we will lose ourselves in outward things, thus seeking vainly for the One Who is all the time within us? If we would be with Him, we may be sure that we shall find Him within us. He is truly there, and we can always find Him and see Him with the eye of faith. He will reward us one day by revealing Himself as He is, without any medium at all. We know, for Saint Paul tells us, that Christ dwells by faith in our hearts.[13] Christ is in faith, faith is in our soul, and our soul is within us. By faith, then, we worship our Creator, adoring our Redeemer and waiting upon our Saviour. By faith we see God in every creature. We possess Him in ourselves, and what is infinitely more blessed, we know Him in Himself.

To know the Father, the Son and the Holy Spirit—this is eternal life, perfect bliss, and highest delight. Eye has not seen, ear has not heard, nor has the heart of any man conceived[14] what brightness, what sweetness, and what joy await us in that vision, when we see God face to face. For He is the light of all those who have been enlightened, and the rest of all those who have come through the fight. He is the homeland of those who have finished their pilgrimage. He is the life of the living, and the crown of those who triumph.

As we have already seen, there is in every soul a little trinity of memory, knowledge and love, wherewith each one of us may recollect God's benefits, look upon Him with sure knowledge, love, embrace and contemplate Him. All our living is in these three, since all that we know belongs to the memory (which is an image of God the Father); to the reason it belongs to seek the good and the true (thus imaging the Son), and as for the will, or love, nothing could bear more resemblance to the Holy Spirit. Love is the highest gift of God, and is God Himself under the form of gift. As Saint Paul says, 'God's love has been poured into our hearts through the Holy Spirit which has been given to us.'[15] And in this way, the whole Trinity lives within us.

CHAPTER 4

THE PROMISE OF ETERNAL LIFE

OUR reward in heaven is to see God, to live with God, and to live with the very life of God. It is to be with God, and to be in God, Who will be all in all. We shall possess God, the highest good. Where the highest good is, there is the highest joy, the supremest happiness, the truest liberty, the most perfect charity. There we shall find eternal security, fullest knowledge, and all that is blissful and beautiful.

In this wise, man will be happy with God. His utmost desire of seeing God will be fulfilled, and his rejoicing will have no end. Henceforth there can be no stain on his conscience, but he will shine with truth. He will be full of wisdom, full of rest, and his eyes will be forever on his Lord. He will be a citizen of heaven, and a fellow citizen with saints and angels. God the Father will be his temple, God the Son will be his splendour, and God the Holy Spirit will be his love.

O heavenly city, O blessed citizens! What glorious things are said of you![16] All are rejoicing there at the sight and sound of God's beauty. He is delightful to see and sweet to possess. He is all our reward, and beyond Him there is nothing further to desire. He is the whole of man's good, in this life and the next, for to know and love God is the highest good we may ever attain.

Why, then, can we be so mad as to thirst after the wormwood of this world? Why do we follow in the wake of this world's shipwreck? Why do we allow ourselves to be lorded over by a cruel and evil tyrant? Why do we not fly away, here and now, to the company of the angels and the happiness of the saints? Why should we not give ourselves up to the enjoyment of heavenly happiness, the joy of the contemplative life, so that we may enter into the power of the Lord,[17] and see the superabundant riches of His goodness? For there we shall find rest, and see how gracious the Lord is. We shall know the blessed Trinity in the might of the Father, the wisdom of the Son, and the untold mercy of the Holy Spirit.

In this life we look upon bodily things with our bodily eyes, and thereby see images of these same bodies by means of our spiritual powers. But we shall see the holy Trinity by present insight. O blessed vision, O to see God in Himself and in ourselves, and ourselves in Him! Whatever we see we shall love, with the love of the blessed, with the sweetness of contemplation. The hidden divinity will be revealed to us, and this vision, filling the heart of man to satiety, will be the consummation of our joy.

There will be one unanimous voice of praise, one object of eternal love. Truth will be revealed and love will be fulfilled. Body and soul will be fully united, and glorified humanity will shine like the sun. Flesh and spirit will be in perfect harmony. Love will not languish, nor affection fade. There where all things are present, there will be no sorrow of departing. The beatifying presence of the divine majesty will be all in all. For all, there will be one wisdom, one understanding, one omnipotence, one peace, one justice. In that peace there will be no diversity of tongues, but an absolute harmony in the affections and actions of all the blessed. In such an abundance and overflowing of delight, all will be filled with enjoyment and bathed in glory.

CHAPTER 5

THE PERFECT CHRISTIAN

BUT which of us is fit to receive such fulness of joy? Surely only he who is truly penitent and humbly obedient; only he who is a faithful servant of his Lord, and a loving and lovable friend to his fellow-men.

A true penitent is he who weeps over his past sins, and strives to avoid future falls. Thus he is ever sorrowing and labouring, for true penance allows no minute to go by without a sigh for past misdeeds. He weeps for the sins he has committed, so that he may refrain from committing those acts which would give him cause for further weeping. It is the merest mockery of penance to persist in doing the evil which causes us to sorrow. If, therefore, you would be a true penitent, cease forthwith from sinning. For that is an empty penance which is sullied by further sin.

Humbly obedient is he who gives his will to good, and his refusal to evil, so that he may say 'My heart is ready, O God, my heart is ready.'[18] Ready, that is, to do all that Thou wilt command, O God; ready to obey Thy least behest, ready to wait upon Thee, to minister to Thy servants, to be vigilant about my own conduct, and to rest in the contemplation of Thy majesty.

A loving and lovable friend is he who is ready and willing to help everyone, and is a burden to no one. He is kind and helpful to others because he is devoted to God, and sober in respect of worldly things. Thus he is a true servant to his Lord, a friend to his fellows, and master over the goods of this world. The One who is above him is his joy, the one who is beside him is his company, and all things beneath him are for his service. He is burdensome to no one, using as he does all things for the usefulness of men and for the honour of his Lord. He follows the rule laid down from above, and draws with him the lesser things which are for his use. He is possessed by heaven, and himself possesses the earth. If a poor man stands at his door, he is sure to let him in for he knows him to be a brother. All men are his own blood kindred since all are brought to life in the blood of our Redeemer.

He is a faithful servant, both in the contemplation of God and in self-custody. We must look after our souls with all care, so that we may realize how impossible it is for us to do so by means of our own unaided efforts. Thereupon we must implore God to help us with His divine mercy. Likewise, in order to know what is God's will for us, we must pray for the guidance of the angel who guards us, and for the intercession of all the saints who reign with Christ in heaven.

If you would be a true penitent, an obedient servant of your Lord, and a loving friend to your fellow-men, seek diligently into the state of your soul by examining your life day by day. Note carefully what progress you make, and what your failures are. Examine your habits and your affections. Strive to see how like God you are, and how unlike Him; how near you are to Him, and how far. Seek, in a word, to know yourself. It is better and more praiseworthy to know yourself, than to neglect yourself while studying the stars in their courses, the virtues of plants and the nature of animals.

Turn to yourself, and if you cannot always do this, at least do it often. And if you cannot often turn to yourself, at the very least do so from time to time. Control your affections, direct your acts and correct your faults. Let nothing in you remain undisciplined, and let your former transgressions be ever before your eyes. Examine yourself with as much detachment as you would examine another. Weep over yourself for the sins you have committed, lamenting to God Whom you have offended. And as you weep for your own soul, do not forget in your charity to weep also for mine.

Since I have known you, brother, I have loved you in Christ, and do love you. When I am at the altar I remember you, for whereas the remembrance of wrong-doing is a torture, the thought of you is a worthy one and as such will bring a reward. I stand at God's altar, a sinner, but still a priest, and my memory commits you to me. If you love me, you will do the same for me, and give me a share in your prayers. For I would be present to you, wherever you are. Whenever you are praying to God for your loved ones and yourself, I would be present in your thoughts. Do not be surprised when I say that I wish to be present. Do you not love me because I am an image of God? Then, since you are likewise His image, I am as present to you as you are to yourself. Whatsoever you are substantially, that also am I. Every rational soul is an image of God, therefore whoever looks for God's image in himself, seeks not only himself but also his neighbour and friend. He who finds the object of his search within himself, finds the same image in all men.

Our mind is the eye of our soul, and when you know and see yourself, you know and see me, for I am none other than yourself. If you love God, then surely you love me who am an image of Him, just as I, loving God, love you. And thus, while we both strive towards God, the one object of our love, we are always present one to another. We are present together in God, in Whom we love each other.

CHAPTER 6

ON PRAYER

WHEN you go into church to pray or sing the hours, leave all the burden of your thoughts at the church door. Forget all outward care, so that you may wait utterly upon God. It is impossible to speak with God when one is already holding converse with the world at large. Look up, then, to the One Who has looked down to you. Listen to Him as He speaks to you, and He will hear and grant your prayer when you pray to Him. Sing His praises with reverence and attend to every word of the psalms and scriptures, and He will not fail to bless you.

I am not saying this as one who is always duly attentive, but I say it since this is the way I desire to pray. When I have not fulfilled this duty as I should, I regret it afterwards. If I am conscious of it at the time, I am ashamed. But to you a greater grace is given, and therefore incline God's ear to yourself with prayers devoutly said. With tears and sighs beg Him to forgive you your sins. In all His works praise Him and glorify Him. How happy we would be if we could see how the most high King is reverenced by the angels, joined with singers and those who play on timbrels! But we can see with the eye of faith that the angels who sing in the choirs of heaven, are not slow to come down to us who pray on earth, to help us in meditation and contemplation, and in our work and daily cares. We are the fellow-citizens of these heavenly powers, and they rejoice with us whose heritage is salvation. They strengthen, guide and comfort us in all our need. They wait upon our coming, since it is we who are to repair the ruin that was once done in their heavenly country.

Therefore the angels seek to hear good report of us, rejoicing when that wish is satisfied. They take our prayers to God and bring His grace down to us. They are made our ministers, and they do not disdain to be counted among our friends. They rejoice over us when we are converted to do penance for our sins. Let us not be slow then to give them the pleasure in which they take so much delight. Woe to any man who would prefer to return to his evil ways, for he cannot suppose that he will have the angels on his side at the day of judgement, if he has denied them the happiness which is theirs by right. They exulted when we turned from our wickedness, seeing in us those who have been called back from the gates of hell. What would be their sorrow if they saw us turning away from the gate of paradise, when we already had one foot in heaven?

Let us run, then, not depending on the strength of our legs, but on the depth of our affections and the vehemence of our desire for God. The angels are not alone in waiting for our arrival in heaven. The creator of the angels is Himself there to welcome us. God the Father is calling us as sons to our inheritance, for He wishes to place us over all His goods. The Son of God calls us as brothers to share in His heritage; He welcomes us as the fruit of His nativity, and as the prize which was bought by His precious blood, offered to the Father. The Holy Spirit waits upon our coming for He is the charity and benignity in which we were for all time predestined, nor is there any doubt as to God's wish to fulfil the promise of predestination.

Therefore, since all the court of heaven is waiting for us, and is desirous of our coming, let us reciprocate their desire with all our heart's longing. He whose conversation is already in heaven by means of continual prayer, will leave this world with a tranquil mind, and will be received in the world to come with great rejoicing. Wherever you are, then, pray in your heart. If you are far from the oratory, do not seek a place to pray in, for you are yourself an oratory—pray there, in your heart. Even if you are lying on your bed, simply pray, and you are in the temple. The mind must be lifted up to God when the body is at rest, and this is done by frequent prayer. There should never be a moment in which God is absent from the memory, because there is never a moment in which we are denied His goodness and mercy.

But perhaps you will say, 'I pray daily, yet my prayer bears no fruit. I see no result of it. I come away from my prayer in exactly the same state as when I approached it. I hear no voice. I get no answer. I am given no gift and my labour seems vain.' Such words are typical of our human frailty, for we take no heed to our Lord's promise: 'Amen I say to you.... Whatever you ask in prayer, you will receive, if you have faith.'[19]

So do not despise your poor prayers, for the One to Whom they are addressed never despises them. Before you have finished uttering the words, He has ordered that they be written down in His book. One of two things we must hope for without doubting—either that He will give us that which we ask, or that which He knows will do us more good. We must think all that is good of God, and all that is bad of ourselves. And we must believe more good of Him than we can even think. All the time in which you are not thinking about God you can count as wasted, for time, unlike other things, is truly in our possession. Every time and every place is suitable for thinking about God. Wherever you may be, give all your thought to Him. Do not be given over to other things, but remain always in possession of your soul, at every time and in every place meditating on things which lead to salvation.

Gather every faculty of your soul into the midst of your heart, and there prepare a fine large place where you can welcome Christ as your guest and spend all your days with Him in perfect freedom. The mind of a wise man is always on God. We must always have Him before our eyes for He it is in Whom we live and have, not only our being, but also our wisdom. He gives the inner delight which draws us on to eternal blessedness. In three things—namely in the being and the wisdom which God grants us, and in the goodness which we experience within our souls, we find an image of the Trinity. God is being and wisdom and goodness. We in our little way have being, and we have knowledge of our being. Our gratitude for these two gifts makes us love God.

The fact that inwardly we are like God must remind us to treat ourselves as true temples of God. To venerate and love God is the highest honour we can do Him, and we imitate Him in reciprocating His love. We do Him reverence by being merciful, even as He is merciful. An acceptable sacrifice to God is to do good to all men for His sake. If we do everything as sons of God, we will become worthy of being called true sons of God. Therefore we must remember God's presence in every act of our lives. God sees all that we do, and therefore we must never offend Him. If we are prepared to find Him everywhere, we may always be sure of His love. Indeed, He is everywhere, either to give us His grace or His punishment. Woe to us if He is present to punish, but greater woe if He gives neither grace nor punishment, for the sinner whom He does not chastise in this life will surely be damned in the next.

CHAPTER 7

THE INCONSTANCY OF THE HUMAN HEART

It is certain that death threatens us everywhere. The devil prepares with all his wiles to take the soul when it leaves the body. But none need fear if God lives in his soul. God will save him from death and the devil. He is a faithful friend, and He never deserts those who hope in Him, unless they have already deserted Him. When we allow our hearts to wander after unworthy and useless things, we are forgetting God and departing from Him. Therefore, if anyone would find his ultimate rest in God, let him take care to remain always with God, and keep God's presence with him. Of all the creatures under the sun which busy themselves with the vanities of this life, none is more deluded than the human heart, for none is more noble or more akin to God. That is why God asks nothing of us but our heart. We must cleanse our heart with pure confession and persevering prayer if we would be brought to the sight of Him.

Love all men, and be lovable to all, so that you may be a peacemaker and a true son of God. You will be humble and holy then, and more than ever I shall beg your prayers, for I, who am speaking of what a man ought to do to please God, act so rarely in a way that can please Him. What little good I have ever done I have not persevered in. I know well enough what is right, but to judge by my conduct you would not think so. I can speak of what is good and right without doing it. I can ponder the law of God in my heart and still transgress the law. I can read about holy things and yet prefer reading to prayer. Holy scripture speaks to me of the love of God, of charity, of the unity of Christian brotherhood—and I would willingly read, yet less willingly assist at mass, or strive after contemplation.

May God have mercy on me, for I multiply sins when I should be trying to amend. So often I pray with my mind absent from my prayer. But it is of little use to sing to God with a voice unaccompanied by an attentive mind. How can I presume to call so often on God's majesty, while turning my ears away from Him the next instant to things which are futile? Surely the Creator of the universe must one day punish this little dust which turns away from Him when He has deigned to listen to it. And yet, God looks down every day upon our hard hearts and deaf ears, and still He calls to us, 'Come back to My heart.'[20]

There is nothing in me as elusive as my heart. It is undependable, inconstant, given to vanity and wandering as long as it follows its own sweet will. And when it is like this it is offensive to God, and it is little wonder that it lacks God's consolation. My heart is virtually incapable of staying in any one place. It is distracted by many, many things; it rushes in this direction and that, more volatile than anything you can think of. It is seeking for rest in many different things and so, of course, it cannot find anywhere that which it most needs. Wretchedness accompanies all its endeavours, and it is forever empty of what it would cherish most. It is at odds with itself, and disgusted with itself, for its wishes are not five minutes the same. It will build up a house of ambitious dreams and tear it down again. It will build again, and destroy again, and hanker after utterly contrary things at the same moment.

The heart's desires go round and round like the sails of

a windmill. It seizes upon anything as grist, and if nothing is offered it will consume itself. Ever in motion, never at rest, my heart grinds away at the memory of past days and the thought of present and future ones. They say that if sand gets into the millstones it will bring them to a halt. Straw, likewise, will block them up and any dirt in the stones will spoil the flour. My heart is made foul by impure thoughts, put out of gear by anger and bitterness, and wearied to no purpose by dwelling on things which are of no importance.

But as long as my heart takes no thought for its eternal joy and peace, and as long as it is prepared to ignore the divine help in seeking for blessedness, it can only find itself ever more distant from God as it loses itself in worldly occupations. Curiosity draws it further away from God. Covetousness and pleasure seduce it, sensuality befouls it. It is twisted by envy, shattered by anger, and tortured by sadness. Having abandoned the one God Who is sufficient to it, it can only drown in all manner of vices and sorrows.

It can find nothing to satisfy all its craving until it returns to the consideration of itself. Then it sees all its thoughts and desires as the mere nothings they are. The imagination has become a deceiver, and the devil has fed it with illusions. 'Let God teach me,' cries the heart at last, 'let God teach me to give myself to Him wholly. I have disobeyed Him and gone against the law of my own nature, created by God. How can I obey this law unless I subject myself to God? I am not united to God, and it is for this reason that I am, in myself, divided. I cannot be made one with Him except through charity, nor can I obey Him without humility, nor can I be truly humble unless I know the truth about Him and about myself.'

Thus I learn—for it is expedient for me to learn—how

weak and how unworthy I am. When I am truly familiar with the depths of my own wretchedness, I must cleave to Him Who is the whole reason for my being, and without Whom I cannot exist, let alone act, for one moment. I made my journey away from God by sinning. I cannot return to Him without a true confession of all the evil I have done.

CHAPTER 8

AN EXAMINATION OF CONSCIENCE

I MUST confess . . . all that is to be confessed. But I have forgotten so much. There were sins I committed long ago, and other sins so often repeated that their number is past my counting. There have been times when I was stupid enough to divide my confession between two or even three confessors, so as not to risk overwhelming any one priest with the full tale. I have made superficial confessions when there was need to probe more deeply into my conscience. Confession is of little avail unless there is truth in the mouth and purity of intention in the heart. Just as there are three who give witness in heaven, the Father, the Son, and the Holy Spirit, so on earth may one discern three witnesses through whom every matter may be established—namely our heart, our mouth, and our confessor's ear.

If anyone objects that it suffices for the sinner to confess his sin to God, since without God no priest can absolve the penitent, my answer is that of Saint James . . . 'confess your sins one to another.'[21] One can urge, moreover, that God did not withhold the mediatorship of Christ the man to bring us to salvation. Therefore it seems right and just that we should turn to the Mediator in His priests in order to return to Him. The man who has chosen not to bow down before his creator will do well to bow down to our Mediator Christ. On his knees let him weep and ask pardon. Let him repent from the heart and make confession to God and man with the words of his mouth. For it is God Who deigns to come down to the sinner's heart, giving him compunction. Let the sinner, then, come to meet his God Who is thus condescending towards him, that he may receive pardon for his sins.

In the past I have preferred that God should be ignorant of my sin—as if that were possible. I have pretended to myself that I could avoid punishment. I have wished God to be ignorant, unjust and powerless. In a word, I have wished that God were not God. But now I will not deny that I am a sinner. I know and confess my sin, and therefore I dare hope for pardon of a kindly judge. I will tell Him of all my wretchedness, and He will be moved to forgiveness, seeing that this recognition of my sin in confession is the beginning of my salvation.

If I dared not look into my conscience I would remain in ignorance about myself, but now that I look within my soul, I am appalled by what I see. The deeper I look, the more terrible are the things I find. I have not ceased to sin, from the moment when my first sin was committed long ago; nor do I cease to sin now. I am so used to sinning that I can look on the evil I have done without sorrow or tears. That alone is like a sign of damnation. When one of the members of the body is without feeling, it is sometimes a sign that it is already moribund. One cannot cure an illness of which one is unconscious.

I am dissolute and irresponsible, but I will not correct myself, and so I continue to commit the sins I have already confessed. I take no heed of the pit into which I have already once fallen, or seen others fall, or even helped them to fall, which is worse. I should be weeping and praying for all my past misdeeds, but I am cold and insensible. There is no more fervour left in my prayer. I cannot shed the least tear in contrition, for even the grace of tears has left me.

Help me then, O God, for my enemies have surrounded my soul on every side. Wherever I look, I find the world, the flesh and the devil. From the flesh I cannot take refuge, nor can it depart from me until it is called away by Thee. I must carry it with me everywhere for we are bound together. To destroy it is not lawful; to sustain it is a duty. Yet if I take good care of it I am only giving strength to my enemy. Then there is the world to beset me at each one of my five senses. Through these it aims its sharp arrows, and death follows them into my very soul. What I see, what I hear, what I touch—all these things are so often an incitement to evil, and if their suggestions are not forthwith rejected, the whole body is soon on fire with temptation.

The devil sets his snares in silver and gold. Like birds we are caught in the trap of covetousness and the love of possessions. The love of our loved ones, the honours which we are offered, the pleasures of the flesh—all these are the devil's birdlime, wherewith he holds fast the wings of our souls so that they cannot fly up in contemplation to the heavenly city. The days of man are like a shadow on the earth, and nothing is enduring. Why, then, do men store up treasures here below, since all treasure is as fleeting as those who hoard it? What profit can we have of a world whose end is death?

Save me from my enemies, O God, and from the hand of all those who hate me, for they have grown strong at my expense. Until this day I have lived at variance with myself and with my soul's desires, but now I begin to live through Thy grace. In this life we must learn to live with the true knowledge that when the soul is rejoicing with the saints in heaven, the body in its tomb is food for worms. And so the spirit must look up in the direction in which it is to take its last journey. We must be hastening to heaven because it is there that we shall live for ever. If we have any love for the present life, with all its failings, its labours, its burdens and necessities, how much more must we love that eternal life where there is no hardship, but only highest joy, fullest freedom? There the blessed spirits of the just rejoice with the angels of God. What will the splendour of their souls be when their bodies in the light of glory are shining like the sun?

CHAPTER 9

THE OLD MAN AND THE NEW

O SOUL of man, and glorious image of God! Are you not made beautiful in His likeness? Are you not espoused to Him by faith? Has He not given you His Spirit as your marriage portion? Has He not redeemed you in His blood? Has He not given you a place among the angels, with salvation for your inheritance? Has He not gifted you with reason and destined you for eternal happiness?

Why, then, will you suffer together with the flesh? Why do you burden yourself with the sins of that which is below you? Why will you conspire with the flesh in dooming yourself to a share in its destruction? How long will you persist in adorning yourself with things of little worth which this world holds precious, when you can put on the beauty of good deeds and so be made fit to appear with the angels in heaven? Why do you count yourself of so little worth, and give the flesh an esteem it could never merit? Why do you allow yourself to be browbeaten by your servant, when it is you who should be commanding him?

A single soul is of more value than all else in the universe. Our Lord did not lay down His life for the world, but for you. The precious blood of Christ is the price He paid for you, and you are willing to give yourself away in exchange for things of no worth at all. It was for you that the Son left the bosom of the Father. He came down to save you from the devil's snares, and from the eternal death which otherwise you could not have avoided. He wept over you when you knew not how to weep for your own sad state.

Look at yourself now, and see how noble a creature you are. Look at the deep wounds of Christ and think how deeply you yourself were wounded by sin, that Christ should be so used for your sake. Forget what the flesh bids you to do, and listen to what God commands. Go back to God and you will be glorious again. Remember that there have been many who loved the world, and these have long since returned to dust. If only we would look to the last things, and have understanding! If only we could see that the old man has lived familiarly with us for years, seated at our table, sleeping in our breast, and conversing with us every day. Once he was our servant, but we have nurtured him so delicately, and spared him the rod so effectively, that he has become stronger than ourselves, and reduced us to the position of his servant. If only we could see how he tyrannizes over us, with his one criterion of that which is earthly, with his blindness and deafness to the things of the spirit!

He would rob us of our inheritance and trample us in the dust. Meanwhile he plays with us, and flatters us, but only so that he may trip us up the more easily when he thinks fit. All the time, the contest is within us. The devil's servant, the lover of this world, the contemnor of God—these are all the same old man within us. What is to be done with him? Would you not agree that he is worthy of death, even the death of the cross? This is no time to spare him. You must judge him now, and quickly. You must crucify him on the cross of Christ, in which is our life and our salvation. And if you will call on our crucified Lord, He will answer you lovingly, 'To-day you will be with Me in paradise,'[22] for it is yourself whom you are crucifying. Such is the love of Christ—great and gratuitous, patient, benign and merciful. At one minute you were in the lion's mouth, but now you are in the Mediator's arms. One minute at the gates of hell, the next in paradise.

But of what use are all these words which I have written unless I strike out from my own conscience the letters which spell death? What is the profit in writing, reading and understanding, unless we look to ourselves, and read and understand our souls? To read ourselves is to love God, and to fight against our enemies, the world, the flesh, and the devil.

CHAPTER 10

THE INNER HOUSE OF CONSCIENCE

THERE are, indeed, many sciences to be found among men, but none is better than a man's knowledge of himself. For my part I will go into my heart and learn to remain there, so that I may pass judgement on my whole life, and that I may know myself. Self-knowledge is the highest knowledge, and those who have it and keep it will always be secure. With all due respect for wisdom, it is true to say that a man may seek self-knowledge more profitably than wisdom, unless it be the wisdom which builds up conscience, the house of self-knowledge.

When the conscience is enlightened, the soul knows itself. It is a good conscience which not only sees itself in God, but sees in itself the created image of God. The creating image in the created image is none other than wisdom in the soul, holiness in the ark of the covenant, the light of glory in the soul's self-knowledge. What ineffable love is it which induces the very majesty of God to come down to such lowliness? He Who created us is created in us. As if it were not sufficient for Him to be our Father, He wishes to be our mother and brother besides. As our mother He gives us birth; as our brother He is obedient to us, and shares with us His own inheritance.

Since this is so, let us open our hearts to Him; let us enlarge the power of our love. He Whom the whole world cannot contain will not be born of us if our capacity for receiving Him is mean and narrow. The Blessed Virgin conceived Him by her faith, and likewise is He conceived within us. He is born of us through the preaching of His word; He is fed on our devotion and kept close to us by love. Let our conscience, then, be pure, so that it may lead God to the hospitality which our soul offers Him. Let it come to Him with humble service and surround Him with care and attention, so that the infinite majesty of God may not be disinclined to visit our hearts. Such a conscience is the soul's rejoicing for it is wholly at peace with itself, reverent to men and angels, and pleasing to God.

Self-knowledge, or conscience, is knowledge of the heart. This means, firstly, that knowledge which the soul acquires about itself through reflecting on itself; and secondly, all knowledge of other things which it obtains through knowledge of itself. The soul's inner knowledge of itself is its conscience, and the rest is science. There is no possession more valuable than a good conscience. None is more securely kept. None grants more happiness. A good conscience is a dwelling-place for the Holy Spirit, a temple of Solomon, a garden of delight. It is that closed book which will be opened on the day of judgement. However much the body may burden us, or the world betray us, or the devil strike us with fear, conscience remains always unperturbed, for it will be secure when the soul is separated from the body. The world goes on its usual way with laughing and weeping, and at last it must pass and perish, but conscience is undismayed. The body may be given over to scourging and suffering, but no such things as these may threaten conscience.

In the mirror of conscience a man may discover both his internal and external state. The soul has no other mirror than its conscience, and the better the conscience the clearer the mirror. A woman who seeks to please her husband or her lover, will gaze into her mirror in order to beautify the face she sees there. The soul likewise looks into the mirror of conscience to read there and to mark the traces of the creator's image becoming clearer and clearer. In its conscience, the eye of reason may see exactly what is becoming or unbecoming about itself. And God admonishes it thus: O wise heart! O heart excelling in every gift—why are you engaged in so many vain and futile things? It is not right that you should thus minister to such trifles, for you were meant to be their master. These things need you, so that they may have some reason for their existence. Whereas you need them, neither for your blessedness nor for your immortal life. If your servant the body should exceed the bounds of necessity, it is destroying itself by means of the very things which were designed to help it.

Man's conscience is the Lord's vineyard. It is cultivated with confession of sins, satisfaction for sins, good works and perseverance therein. Or again, conscience is like a book. Each man has his own, and all the books in the world are written only for the amending of the book of conscience. When the soul leaves the body, it may take nothing with it except that book. Reading there, it will know whither it must go and what reward it is about to receive. For we shall be judged upon all that is written in our book, and therefore we must be sure that we have a faithful copy of the Book of Life. Let each one of us compare his book with the Book of Life, and correct it accordingly, so that at its last reading none of us may be excluded for being found to read otherwise than he should.

CHAPTER 11

THE SEVEN PILLARS OF WISDOM

WHEN Wisdom sets about building her house, she first raises up seven pillars to carry the weight of the whole structure.[23] The house which Wisdom builds is conscience, and the pillars are these: the first is goodness of will, and the second is the memory of God's benefits. The third is a pure heart, and the fourth is freedom, both of heart and mind. The fifth is a Godward spirit, the sixth is devotion, and the seventh contemplation.

Of all the gifts which God has bestowed upon mankind for his salvation, the first and chiefest is that of a good will by means of which the image of God is restored in us. It is first because the soul is incapable of good if it has not goodness in the will. It is the chiefest because God never gave a man anything which could be more useful to him. Whatever a man does, it cannot be good unless it comes from the goodness of his will. Without a good will none can be saved, but with a good will no man can perish. It cannot be given to anyone who is not desirous of it, nor can it be taken away without a man first consent to losing it. The will of man is the power of God. All meriting is in the will, and we merit in so far as we use our will. As the will increases in goodness, merits likewise increase. Let a man, then, make himself a great good will if he would have great merit. God, most loving and merciful Father that He is, put our redemption in that which no man lacks, unless he be fool enough to wish it lacking. For all men possess the power of loving in equal measure, and the will is not good unless it does its proper work, which is love.

Now if we would seek to be set on fire with the love of God, we must remember His mercies towards us. Let us bring to mind the good things He has bestowed on us. Let us remember how often He has deigned to snatch us from danger, and how He has never failed to pity us in our sins. He has admonished those who had forgotten Him, and called back to Himself those who had turned away from Him. Those who have returned to Him He has received with every kindness. He has pardoned the penitent, and kept from danger those who have amended their ways. He has raised up the fallen, and those who stand upright owe their steadfastness only to Him. He has turned sinful pleasure into bitterness and given His own consolation in place of both. He has given peace and perfect rest to those whom tribulation has purified. He never abandons the soul of a sinner, but is ever watchful for an opportunity to turn him away from sin. Neither is He ever absent from the souls of the just, so that He may keep them safely.

Let us recollect how much good God has done to us at times when, far from seeking His goodness, we had no desire for Him, and were even turned away from Him. How many sins He has forgiven us! How many times has He saved us from the snare! How greatly has His fatherly love deigned to come down to us, ungrateful and recalcitrant as we are! How often has His grace kept us from sinning! And so, just as God at no time leaves us without the enjoyment of His kindness and mercy, so should we at all times keep Him present with us in our memory.

It then follows that we should love God with all our heart, since we have received such benefits from Him, and with all our love and all our thought in constancy. In order to please God our heart must be upright in virtue of our soul's intention, to the exclusion of all perversity of thought. Our heart must be assiduous in contemplating God. It must be ready to follow Him in whichever direction it knows God's will is leading. It must tend upward to heavenly things for all its contemplation and all its desiring. It must be pure, allowing no evil thing to remain within it. It must not come to tolerate the least offensive thing, either in its own conscience or in another's. Let the heart give kind answers to kind words, let it reprove benignly, correct others with moderation, and be humble when it is itself reproved. Let it spew out all impurity and let it weep for its sins, both of thought and action. Let it sorrow for its own misery and for that of others.

Let the soul be free of all worldly care, free from the pleasures of the flesh and from lewd thoughts, so that it may at will either look to itself, or minister to the needs of the brethren, or rest quietly in heavenly contemplation. It must be steadfast, so as not to be caught by false allurements or upset by sudden distress or broken down by troubles. No anger, no impatience must trouble the soul's peace, for our peace is Christ; He is the great lover of peace, and in peace He rests. If our soul is at rest, Christ the lover of peace is at rest with us. He cannot stay in a soul which is full of commotion. When the soul is quite free, it can be quite consumed in the love of God. And to love God is to be wholly occupied with God.

Our spirit must be turned towards God, and away from all present and earthly things. It must be inseparably joined to God and made one with Him. The spirit must rise up on wings of devotion so as to find its way about in heaven. There it will bow down before the Lamb on His throne, and will tread all the ways of Zion. It will hear the melodies which angels make, and will make supplication to all the hierarchy of blessed spirits for all men on earth. Such graces as these evidently cannot come upon a soul unless it is well exercised in self-knowledge and thoroughly well acquainted with the truth about itself. The eye of the heart looks up in vain, unless it is used to looking at the truth about itself. Before we are given to know the invisible things of God, we must be acquainted with that invisible thing which is our spirit. The first and chiefest mirror in which we see God is the mirror which our own spirit sees when it looks for the first time at itself. If the invisible things of God are made known through those which are visible, where else, I ask you, than in God's image, are you to find traces of Him more apparent, even to your eyes? If anyone seeks God, let him but polish that mirror. Let him but seek to have his soul cleansed, and his thirst for God shall indeed be satisfied.

'Blessed are the pure of heart for they shall see God.'[24] A true penitent will look into this mirror day by day without fail, rubbing it clean and looking after it with the greatest care. He looks into it to find if there is anything there which might displease God. He polishes it—that is to say, he rubs away the least thing which might offend God, not only in the way of sinful acts but also of sinful thoughts. He holds it well up in order to keep it from the dust of idle thoughts, and from reflecting only those things which belong to the earth. He looks after it so that God, Who has taken up His dwelling with men and Whose delight is to be with the sons of men, may find in his spirit a not unworthy place whenever He comes and knocks at the door. God is the great lover of purity and He cannot live in an impure heart. Learn to live in your heart, and let it be the dwelling in which you love best to be. If you are distracted by external care, always go back to your heart as soon as you are able. Habit will make your heart a place of solace and delight for you—so much so that after a time you will find no difficulty at all in finding your way thither. And if you find your desires becoming attached to external pleasures, and all your thoughts engaged thereon, take care to ensure that they do not find their way into your heart. Rather do you give them the slip and go quickly back to your heart and stay there.

A mind which has not yet risen to the consideration of itself, but which still is dispersed by the variety of its desires, cannot collect itself into one simple faculty since it has not yet learned to enter into itself. Therefore it cannot rise by means of the wings of contemplation to things which are above itself. It must first learn to collect its scattered thoughts and desires, and in order to do this it must learn to live within the heart. Let it seek to restrain its wanderings and to forget what is without. Let it love the good it knows inwardly to be beyond all other good, and to think thereon without stint. When the mind has looked thus to itself and discovered what it is, it only remains for divine revelation to make known what it should strive to become.

Whoever will gather all his vagrant thoughts and desires into one single yearning for eternal blessedness, has indeed found his way back to the inner dwelling of his heart, and there he will delight to remain for he will find in it a wondrous joy. And since he will be unable to contain himself with so great a happiness, he will rise up to higher things as his soul flows over in ecstasy. Now that he is made familiar with his soul's state, he will rise up to the knowledge of God, and then he will learn to love God alone, to think forever of God alone, and to rest in the enjoyment of Him.

When the love of Christ has so absorbed all the soul's love into itself, the soul is forgetful of all but its Lord. This, to my way of thinking, is perfect charity. To anyone who is thus affected by the love of God, poverty is no burden, injuries go unnoticed, adversity is matter for rejoicing, the world's condemnation is a thing of no account, and death itself is gain since the soul sees this as a passing over into true life. Anyone who is thus inwardly bound and made captive by the love of God, has no inclination to seek any outward thing, for all its desire is enkindled within. It is the more afire with love for having love dwell so intimately within it. The more often it experiences inward love, the more ardently it burns to give love in return.

Delighting thus constantly in the love of God, the soul will often find itself poured out in an ecstasy of love. It is rapt from all thought of present and earthly things. It is stupefied by the beauty of God, by the glory of the King and of His kingdom. It tastes God's sweetness and rests in His eternal quiet. Silently it dwells on the shining of heaven's incorporeal light, the savour of being deeply filled with God and the hidden things which He reveals to the soul in His silence.

NOTES

[1] Pliny, *Natural History*, Book VII, 32.
[2] Job v. 24.
[3] Cant. i. 7.
[4] Juvenal, Satire 14.
[5] II Cor. iv. 16.
[6] Gen. ii. 7.
[7] Ovid, *Metamorphoses* I, 84–86.
[8] Job v. 7.
[9] Gen. iii. 19.
[10] I Cor. xii. 26.
[11] Gal. v. 16.
[12] Ecclus. xxiv. 12.
[13] Eph. iii. 17.
[14] I Cor. ii. 9.
[15] Rom. v. 5.
[16] Ps. lxxxvii. 3.
[17] Ps. lxx. 16 (Vulgate).
[18] Ps. cviii. 1.
[19] Matt. xxi. 22.
[20] Isa. xlvi. 8 (Vulgate).
[21] Jas. v. 16.
[22] Luke xxiii. 43.
[23] Prov. ix. 1.
[24] Matt. v. 8.